GOD WON'T LEAVE YOU THERE

A Bible Study on the Life of Joseph

Books and Video Bible Studies by Anne Graham Lotz and Rachel-Ruth Lotz Wright

Preparing to Meet Jesus
Jesus Followers: Real-Life Lessons for Igniting Faith in the Next Generation
Jesus Followers (Study Guide and DVD)

Books by Anne Graham Lotz

The Light of His Presence: Prayers to Draw You Near to the Heart of God
Jesus in Me: Experiencing the Holy Spirit as a Constant Companion
The Daniel Prayer: Prayer That Moves Heaven and Changes Nations
Wounded by God's People: Discovering How God's Love Heals Our Hearts
Expecting to See Jesus: A Wake-Up Call for God's People
The Magnificent Obsession: Embracing the God-Filled Life
God's Story
Just Give Me Jesus
Pursuing More of Jesus
Why? Trusting God When You Don't Understand
Heaven: My Father's House (revised)
The Vision of His Glory: Finding Hope Through the Revelation of Jesus Christ

Video Bible Studies by Anne Graham Lotz

Jesus in Me (Study Guide and DVD)
The Daniel Prayer (Study Guide and DVD)
Expecting to See Jesus (Study Guide and DVD)
The Magnificent Obsession (Study Guide and DVD)
God's Story (Study Guide and DVD)
Pursuing More of Jesus (Study Guide and DVD)
Heaven (Curriculum DVD and Children's DVD)
The Vision of His Glory (Study Guide and DVD)

For more resources by Anne Graham Lotz visit
AnneGrahamLotz.org.

GOD WON'T LEAVE YOU THERE

A Bible Study on the Life of Joseph

BIBLE STUDY GUIDE + STREAMING VIDEO

EIGHT SESSIONS

ANNE GRAHAM LOTZ
RACHEL-RUTH LOTZ WRIGHT

God Won't Leave You There Study Guide

Published by HarperChristian Resources, 3950 Sparks Drive SE, Suite 101, Grand Rapids, MI 49546, USA.
HarperChristian Resources is a registered trademark of HarperCollins Christian Publishing, Inc.

Requests for information should be addressed to customercare@harpercollins.com.

ISBN 978-0-310-17832-3 (softcover)
ISBN 978-0-310-17834-7 (ebook)

HarperChristian Resources titles may be purchased in bulk for church, business, fundraising, or ministry use. For information, please email ResourceSpecialist@ChurchSource.com.

The authors are represented by Alive Literary Agency, www.aliveliterary.com.

HarperCollins Publishers, Macken House, 39/40 Mayor Street Upper, Dublin 1, D01 C9W8, Ireland (https://www.harpercollins.com).

Art direction: Ron Huizinga
Cover Design: Thinkpen Design
Interior Design: Thinkpen Design

First Printing January 2026 / Printed in the United States of America

CONTENTS

About Anne Graham Lotz

Called "the best preacher in the family" by her father, Billy Graham, Anne Graham Lotz speaks around the globe with the wisdom and authority of years spent studying God's Word.

The *New York Times* named Anne one of the five most influential evangelists of her generation. She's been profiled on *60 Minutes* and has appeared on TV programs such as *Larry King Live*, *The Today Show*, and *Hannity Live*. Her *Just Give Me Jesus* revivals have been held in more than thirty cities in twelve different countries, with hundreds of thousands of attendees.

Whether a contributor to national newspapers, or a groundbreaking speaker on platforms throughout the world, Anne's aim is clear—to bring revival to the hearts of God's people. And her message is consistent—calling people into a personal relationship with God through His Word and through prayer.

In May 2016, Anne was named the chairperson of the National Day of Prayer Task Force, a position held by only two other women, Shirley Dobson and Vonette Bright, since its inception in 1952.

Anne is a bestselling and award-winning author. Her most recent releases are *The Vision of His Glory, Preparing to Meet Jesus, Jesus Followers, The Light of His Presence, Jesus in Me, The Daniel Prayer, Wounded by God's People, Fixing My Eyes on Jesus, Expecting to See Jesus*, and her children's book, *Heaven: God's Promise for Me.*

Anne and her late husband, Danny Lotz, have three grown children and three grandchildren. She is the founder and president of AnGeL Ministries, an independent, nonprofit organization based in Raleigh, North Carolina, that is committed to giving out messages of biblical exposition so God's Word is personal and relevant to ordinary people.

To learn more about Anne and AnGeL Ministries, visit **annegrahamlotz.org**.

About Rachel-Ruth Lotz Wright

Rachel-Ruth Lotz Wright was born and raised in Raleigh, North Carolina. She is the daughter of Anne Graham Lotz and the granddaughter of Billy Graham. After graduating from Baylor University, she married Steven Wright and they have three daughters.

Rachel-Ruth teaches a weekly women's Bible study that began at the University of North Carolina and now reaches thousands around the world through Zoom. She also shares God's Word at events across the country. In addition, she is the Vice President of AnGeL Ministries and chairs the weekly prayer team that supports her mother's ministry. She has coauthored two books with her mother, *Jesus Followers* and *Preparing to Meet Jesus*.

Rachel-Ruth feels called to encourage others to fall in love with Jesus through the teaching of His Word. To learn more about Rachel-Ruth, visit **annegrahamlotz.org/about-rachel-ruth-lotz-wright**.

PREFACE

You are about to embark on a thrilling adventure as you step into Joseph's Story. Thank you for choosing this study. We believe you are going to be richly blessed.

One of the most beautiful and poignant blessings is that we see a reflection of Jesus Himself in Joseph's life. Jesus, the beloved favored Son, was sent by the heavenly Father to find and save His "brothers." In obedience to His Father, Jesus began a journey that was thirty-three years long.

Although He was in His Father's will, doing the right thing and even going the extra mile all the way to the cross, He, like Joseph, was set on a path of suffering—a path fiercer, the attacks more brutal, and the pain more immense than we could conceive or a human heart could endure. Jesus, too, was rejected by those He sought to redeem, despised by those He loved. He was stripped of His robe, which was not dipped in animal's blood but soaked in His own blood and gambled for by cruel soldiers. His brothers didn't throw Him into a pit; they crucified Him! He was alone. Forsaken.

Yet, like Joseph, in the blink of an eye, Jesus was raised up to sit on a throne! And from that exalted position He was, and still is, able to save not only His family but the entire world, which includes anyone and everyone who comes to Him by faith. One day the whole world will acknowledge His authority as every knee bows before Him. Jesus won't be wearing a seamless robe that was gambled for but a robe of light more brilliant than the sun! He will be the center of universal praise as the One who alone is worthy of all glory, honor, power, strength, and wisdom. In the end, the Father's ultimate purpose is revealed. The Son of the Father is known to the whole world as the Lamb of God whose blood atones for our sin. Jesus will be known as the only Savior whose suffering opens the way for our reconciliation with His Father, as the Risen Lord who one day will rule the world as King of kings.

Could it be that you, like Joseph, are in the process of becoming a reflection of Jesus? If you find yourself on a path of suffering that is made even more painful because you have done nothing wrong, look for Jesus in the shadows. He is with you. He is guiding you. And He will bring you through.

Step into Joseph's story because God won't leave you there. . . .

Every blessing,

Anne Rachel-Ruth

About the Study

This study guide is to be used with the video-based course *God Won't Leave You There: Joseph's Story*. As an integral part of the course, it provides a format for Bible study that serves as the basis for both small-group use (Sunday school classes, women's or men's groups, home or neighborhood studies, one-on-one discipleship) and individual use. This guide will lead you through a series of questions that enables you to not only discover for yourself the eternal truths revealed by God in the Bible, but also to hear God speaking personally to you through His Word. You then will be prepared to participate in a meaningful time of study and discussion with members of your small group.

Individual Study

Each week you will work through five selected passages of Scripture using the 3-Question Study steps you will learn during the workshop in Session 1. Before you meet with your group, be sure to take the time to reflect and record your personal *Live in Obedient Response* statements to share with your group so they can encourage you and hold you accountable. Take some time to read along and listen to a brief teaching from Anne of Jesus in the Shadows each week using the QR code.

You will review the lessons, personal applications, and takeaways at your group meeting before you watch the video from Anne and Rachel-Ruth. After each video lesson, there will be time to share what further insights you have into the life of Joseph as a group.

It is important to complete each individual study before your next group meeting, as this will make the group discussion time fruitful and prepare you for the video presentation. Note that meaningful, daily Bible study will occur if you:

- Set aside a regular time and place for private devotions.
- Pray before beginning the day's assignment, asking God to speak to you through His Word.
- Write out your answers for each step, in sequence.
- Make the time to be still and listen, reflecting thoughtfully on your response in the final step.
- Don't rush—it may take time in prayerful meditation on a given passage to discover meaningful lessons and hear the Spirit's whispers.
- Spiritual discipline is an essential part of growing in your relationship with God through knowing and understanding His Word. So, take your individual study seriously and allow God to speak to you from the Bible.

GROUP STUDY

In Session 1 of *God Won't Leave You There*, you will watch the video workshop and be introduced to the 3-Question Study method used in Sessions 2 through 8 of the individual Bible study. In the following weeks, you will be given some time to share insights from your weekly individual study before you and your group watch the video teaching. Space is provided for you to take notes during the video presentation. After the message, you will then have time to discuss the key concepts with your small group using the questions in this guide.

Note: If you are the facilitator of the group, there are additional instructions and resources provided in the facilitator's guide at the back of this book. This guide will help you structure your meeting time, facilitate discussion time, and lead group members through the key points of the study.

VIDEO SESSION ACCESS

Free streaming video access is included with this study guide. There is a streaming video access code, along with instructions on how to access all of the video sessions, on the inside front cover of this guide. There is also a short video on the HarperChristian Resources YouTube channel available to guide you through your first-time access of the videos at: **https://youtu.be/JPhG06ksOn8**.

Simply go to: **studygateway.com/redeem** to set up your free account, enter your access code, and add this study to your Bible study library. Each time you wish to view a video, simply log in to **studygateway.com/login** and click on the session or study you wish to view. All of your HarperChristian Resources Bible studies with streaming access will be added to your library as you complete more studies and redeem the appropriate codes.

INDIVIDUAL COMMITMENT

Remember that the real growth in this study will happen during your quiet times with God during the week. During the group times, you will have the opportunity to process what you have learned with the other group members, ask questions, and learn from them as you listen to what God is doing in their lives. In addition, keep in mind that the videos, discussions, and activities in this study are simply meant to tune your heart and your spiritual ears to God's voice so that you can live out what He says as you grow closer to Him.

BIBLE STUDY WORKSHOP

This Bible study workshop has a single purpose: to present an approach that will help you learn to listen for God's voice, know Him in a personal relationship, and communicate with Him through His Word. The following information is introduced in detail in the video presentation. Use this section of the study guide as you view the workshop material. Underline key thoughts and take additional notes as you participate in the workshop. (Note that the passages Anne and Rachel-Ruth use as examples in the video workshop are found on pages 4–7.)

WHAT YOU NEED

Before you begin the video workshop for this first session, you will need the following:

- ☐ a Bible
- ☐ this study guide
- ☐ pen or pencil
- ☐ time
- ☐ prayer
- ☐ an open heart

WATCH VIDEO SESSION 1—BIBLE STUDY WORKSHOP (47 MINUTES)

Use the free streaming video access code found on the inside front cover of this study guide, or play the DVD.

Anne and Rachel-Ruth will use this video session to walk you through the following 5 Steps to Bible Study with the three questions that are essential to the Bible Study Workshop. They will illustrate how to do this Bible study with Psalm 23:1–3 (see pages 4–5 in your study guide).

STEPS TO BIBLE STUDY

STEP 1: READ GOD'S WORD *(Look at the passage.)*

The first step is to read the Bible. At the start of each session in this study guide, you will find the Scriptures that you should read during the week. When you have finished reading the passage for the day, move on to Step 2.

STEP 2: WHAT DOES GOD'S WORD SAY? *(List the facts.)*

After reading the passage, make a verse-by-verse list of the outstanding facts. Don't get caught up in the details—just pinpoint the most obvious facts as they appear to you. When you make your list, do not paraphrase the text but use actual words from the passage. Look for the nouns and the verbs.

STEP 3: WHAT DOES GOD'S WORD MEAN? *(Learn the lessons.)*

After reading the passage and listing the facts, look for a lesson you can learn from each fact.

Ask yourself the following questions:

- Who is speaking?
- What is the subject?
- Where is this taking place?

- When did it happen?
- What can I learn from what is taking place or what is being said? It may also help to ask yourself: What are the people in the passage doing that I should be doing? Is there a command I should obey? A promise I should claim? A warning I should heed? An example I should follow?

Focus on spiritual lessons.

STEP 4: WHAT DOES GOD'S WORD MEAN IN MY LIFE? *(Listen to His voice.)*

Although this step will be the most meaningful for you, you can't do it effectively until you complete the first three steps. So, first rephrase the lessons you found in Step 3 and put them in the form of questions you could ask yourself, your spouse, your child, your friend, your neighbor, or your coworker. As you write the questions, listen for God to speak to you through His Word. Don't get hung up on what you don't understand—instead, look for the general principles and lessons that can be learned. Remember not to rush this process. It may take you several moments of prayerful meditation to discover meaningful lessons from the passage of Scripture you are reading and hear God speaking to you. The object is not to "get through it," but to develop your personal relationship with God in order to grow in faith and learn to hear the whispers of the Holy Spirit.

STEP 5: WHAT WILL YOU DO ABOUT WHAT GOD HAS SAID? *(Live in obedient response to God's Word.)*

Read the assigned Scripture passages prayerfully, objectively, thoughtfully, and attentively as you listen for God to speak. Note that He may not speak to you through every verse, but He will speak. When He does, record the verse number (if applicable), what it is that God seems to be saying to you, and your response to Him. You might like to date these pages as a means of not only keeping a spiritual journal but also holding yourself accountable to follow through in obedience. (See pages 4–5 for the example that Anne and Rachel-Ruth demonstrate in the video.)

Afterward, it is your turn to try this method on your own using Psalm 23:4–6 (see pages 6–7).

BIBLE STUDY EXAMPLE

STEP 1 **Read God's Word.** *(Look at the passage.)*	STEP 2 **What Does God's Word Say?** *(List the facts.)*
Psalm 23:1–3	**List the outstanding facts—nouns and verbs. Do not paraphrase.**
1 The LORD is my shepherd, I lack nothing.	**v. 1** The Lord is my Shepherd. I lack nothing.
2 He makes me lie down in green pastures, he leads me beside quiet waters,	**v. 2** He makes me lie down. He leads me beside quiet waters.
3 he refreshes my soul. He guides me along the right paths for his name's sake.	**v. 3** He refreshes.... He guides me along right paths. For His name's sake

STEP 3

What Does God's Word Mean?

(Learn the lessons.)

Is there a lesson or principle to learn from each fact?

v. 1 When I have a personal relationship with the Lord, He takes care of me.

When the Lord is my Lord, my needs are His responsibility.

v. 2 Sometimes God has to make me take a break and rest.

Following Him leads to inner peace and serenity.

v. 3 When He makes me take a break, it's for a purpose.

To stay on the right path in life, I need His guidance.

His name is at stake in my well-being and my walk.

STEP 4

What Does God's Word Mean in My Life?

(Listen to His voice.)

Rephrase the lessons found in Step 3 into questions.

v. 1 Do I have a personal relationship with the Lord?

What do I think He is not responsible for?

v. 2 Do I feel set aside instead of led to rest?

How closely am I following His lead?

v. 3 Am I weary on the inside? Why?

Who or what do I look to for decisions and direction?

Why do I think He would neglect me or make a mistake if His name is at stake in my life?

STEP 5

What Will You Do About What God Has Said?

(Live in obedient response to God's Word.)

When the Lord is my Lord, I do not need to be alarmed when life throws me a curveball. I can trust Him to lead me on the right path.

Date: ______________________________

"YOUR TURN" EXAMPLE

STEP 1 **Read God's Word.** *(Look at the passage.)*	STEP 2 **What Does God's Word Say?** *(List the facts.)*
Psalm 23:4–6	**List the outstanding facts—nouns and verbs. Do not paraphrase.**
[4] Even though I walk through the darkest valley, I will fear no evil, for you are with me; your rod and your staff, they comfort me.	**v. 4**
[5] You prepare a table before me in the presence of my enemies. You anoint my head with oil; my cup overflows.	**v. 5**
[6] Surely your goodness and love will follow me all the days of my life, and I will dwell in the house of the Lord forever.	**v. 6**

STEP 3 **What Does God's Word Mean?** *(Learn the lessons.)*	STEP 4 **What Does God's Word Mean in My Life?** *(Listen to His voice.)*

STEP 5

What Will You Do About What God Has Said?

(Live in obedient response to God's Word.)

Date: ______________________

Turn to the next page for the Session 2 Weekly Schedule.

WEEKLY SCHEDULE

DAY 1	3-Question Study—Genesis 37:2–4
DAY 2	3-Question Study—Genesis 37:5, 9–11
DAY 3	3-Question Study—Genesis 37:13–16
DAY 4	3-Question Study—Genesis 37:23–24, 26–27
DAY 5	3-Question Study—Genesis 37:28, 36
DAY 6	Reflection
DAY 7	Group Discussion and Video Teaching

God Is with You . . . from the Beginning

"For I know the
plans I have for you,"
declares the LORD,
"plans to prosper
you and not to harm
you, plans to give you
hope and a future."

Jeremiah 29:11

PERSONAL STUDY

READ: GENESIS 37

Reading the whole chapter before studying select passages will give you helpful context and insight.

INTRODUCTION

Sometimes God allows us to be in scary, life-threatening situations where He develops our trust in Him. [When this happens,] we must wait to see what He will do.

While Joseph crouched in the cistern, no doubt he could hear his older brother Judah talking with the other brothers. Judah [suggested his own idea of how Joseph's life could be saved] when he saw a caravan of merchants on their way to Egypt. His plan? Sell Joseph to them instead of murdering him. [So] they sold Joseph as a slave for twenty pieces of silver. To make matters even worse, the merchants who bought him were Ishmaelites . . . his own cousins! [Have you ever had family turn on you?]

Life was desperately hard for Joseph, made even harder by the fact that it was family who had betrayed him. He must have felt his life was completely out of control. Shattered. Ruined. Yet every step was actually being orchestrated by God in order to get Joseph to Egypt [. . .] and into the position God ultimately wanted him to be.

Let's step into Joseph's story. . . .

(from *God Won't Leave You There: Joseph's Story*, pp. 17–18)

God Is with You . . . from the Beginning

STEP 1 **Read God's Word.** *(Look at the passage.)*	STEP 2 **What Does God's Word Say?** *(List the facts.)*
Genesis 37:2–4 2 This is the account of Jacob's family line. Joseph, a young man of seventeen, was tending the flocks with his brothers, the sons of Bilhah and the sons of Zilpah, his father's wives, and he brought their father a bad report about them. 3 Now Israel loved Joseph more than any of his other sons, because he had been born to him in his old age; and he made an ornate robe for him. 4 When his brothers saw that their father loved him more than any of them, they hated him and could not speak a kind word to him.	

GOD IS WITH YOU . . . FROM THE BEGINNING

STEP 3
What Does God's Word Mean?
(Learn the lessons.)

STEP 4
What Does God's Word Mean in My Life?
(Listen to His voice.)

STEP 5
What Will You Do About What God Has Said?
(Live in obedient response to God's Word.)

Date: ______________________

God Is with You . . . from the Beginning

STEP 1 **Read God's Word.** *(Look at the passage.)*	STEP 2 **What Does God's Word Say?** *(List the facts.)*
Genesis 37:5, 9–11	
5 Joseph had a dream, and when he told it to his brothers, they hated him all the more.	
9 Then he had another dream, and he told it to his brothers. "Listen," he said, "I had another dream, and this time the sun and moon and eleven stars were bowing down to me."	
10 When he told his father as well as his brothers, his father rebuked him and said, "What is this dream you had? Will your mother and I and your brothers actually come and bow down to the ground before you?"	
11 His brothers were jealous of him, but his father kept the matter in mind.	

GOD IS WITH YOU . . . FROM THE BEGINNING

STEP 3
What Does God's Word Mean?
(Learn the lessons.)

STEP 4
What Does God's Word Mean in My Life?
(Listen to His voice.)

STEP 5
What Will You Do About What God Has Said?
(Live in obedient response to God's Word.)

Date: ______________________

God Is with You . . . from the Beginning

STEP 1 **Read God's Word.** *(Look at the passage.)*	STEP 2 **What Does God's Word Say?** *(List the facts.)*

Genesis 37:13–16

13 . . . and Israel said to Joseph, "As
you know, your brothers are grazing
the flocks near Shechem. Come, I am
going to send you to them."

"Very well," he replied.

14 So he said to him, "Go and see if all
is well with your brothers and with
the flocks, and bring word back to
me." Then he sent him off from the
Valley of Hebron.

When Joseph arrived at Shechem,
15 a man found him wandering
around in the fields and asked him,
"What are you looking for?"

16 He replied, "I'm looking for my
brothers. Can you tell me where they
are grazing their flocks?"

God Is with You . . . from the Beginning

STEP 3

What Does God's Word Mean?

(Learn the lessons.)

STEP 4

What Does God's Word Mean in My Life?

(Listen to His voice.)

STEP 5

What Will You Do About What God Has Said?

(Live in obedient response to God's Word.)

Date: ______________________________

God Is with You . . . from the Beginning

STEP 1 **Read God's Word.** *(Look at the passage.)*	STEP 2 **What Does God's Word Say?** *(List the facts.)*
Genesis 37:23–24, 26–27	
23 So when Joseph came to his brothers, they stripped him of his robe—the ornate robe he was wearing—	
24 and they took him and threw him into the cistern. The cistern was empty; there was no water in it.	
26 Judah said to his brothers, "What will we gain if we kill our brother and cover up his blood?	
27 "Come, let's sell him to the Ishmaelites and not lay our hands on him; after all, he is our brother, our own flesh and blood." His brothers agreed.	

God Is with You . . . from the Beginning

STEP 3

What Does God's Word Mean?

(Learn the lessons.)

STEP 4

What Does God's Word Mean in My Life?

(Listen to His voice.)

STEP 5

What Will You Do About What God Has Said?

(Live in obedient response to God's Word.)

Date: ______________________

God Is with You . . . from the Beginning

STEP 1 **Read God's Word.** *(Look at the passage.)*	STEP 2 **What Does God's Word Say?** *(List the facts.)*
Genesis 37:28, 36 28 So when the Midianite merchants came by, his brothers pulled Joseph up out of the cistern and sold him for twenty shekels of silver to the Ishmaelites, who took him to Egypt. 36 Meanwhile, the Midianites sold Joseph in Egypt to Potiphar, one of Pharaoh's officials, the captain of the guard.	

God Is with You . . . from the Beginning

STEP 3

What Does God's Word Mean?

(Learn the lessons.)

STEP 4

What Does God's Word Mean in My Life?

(Listen to His voice.)

STEP 5

What Will You Do About What God Has Said?

(Live in obedient response to God's Word.)

Date: ______________________________

GOD IS WITH YOU . . . FROM THE BEGINNING

PERSONAL REFLECTION

Record and journal the following from your personal study on how GOD IS WITH YOU . . . FROM THE BEGINNING.

The Scripture that stood out to you:

The lesson that was most meaningful to you:

The commitment you made to Live in Obedient Response to God's Word:

God Is with You . . . from the Beginning

JESUS IN THE SHADOWS

Scan this QR code for a free bonus teaching from Anne.

Read along with Anne as you watch and listen.

The disciples watched in horror as the Father's beloved Son was seized, bound, accused, tried, tortured, and then nailed to a stake of execution. They must have wanted to shout, "Not this! How can this be God's plan?!"

They had to wait three excruciatingly long days before they were stunningly surprised with joy! The Son's death had indeed been God's plan. Because Jesus wasn't their beloved Master and Rabbi only [. . .] He was the Lamb of God, sacrificed on the wooden altar of the cross to make atonement for their sin. They had to wait through three days of grief and horror before He rose from the dead. He was alive! Their sins were all forgiven. Heaven's gates were opened wide.

The way up to the right hand of the Father had been down. Down from glory. Down to earth. Down all the way to death on the cross. But because it was God's plan, it worked, and His plan includes a glorious future for you. Hallelujah! God's plans always come together!

(from *God Won't Leave You There: Joseph's Story*, p. 19)

GROUP STUDY

WELCOME TO SESSION TWO of the *God Won't Leave You There* study!

NOTE: *You just completed your first week of Personal Bible Study. If the 3-question study technique was new to your group, consider taking a few moments sharing thoughts on the experience before you dive into this week's video teaching. If anyone has questions or concerns about the personal study time, it is likely someone else feels the same way. Spend the time now to find resolution and answers together, so the remainder of this study can be productive and fruitful for everyone.*

Before we watch the video lesson, let's spend some time discussing and sharing what we learned in our personal studies this past week.

Together, refer to Personal Study days 1–5 on pages 12–21.

From Step 3 (for each day)—What lesson did you learn?

From Step 4 (for each day)—What application questions did you ask yourself?

Share one "Live in Obedient Response to God's Word" to which you committed to this week.

Refer to your Personal Reflection on page 22.

WATCH VIDEO SESSION 2— GOD IS WITH YOU . . . FROM THE BEGINNING

(22 MINUTES)

Use the free streaming video access code found on the inside front cover of this study guide, or play the DVD. Use this space to take notes if you like.

Anne and Rachel-Ruth share the beginning of Joseph's story while spending time at the Museum of the Bible in Washington, DC.

Scripture in This Session

Genesis 37

Use this space to take notes if you like.

WRAP-UP

SHARE AS A GROUP

From the video, what was either:

a new thought __________

or a challenge __________

or an encouragement __________

or a blessing __________

CLOSING PRAYER

Lord of Eternity,

I worship You as One who is omniscient. You know everything. You know the beginning . . . and the end. You are the One who is omnipresent. You are with us 24/7. And You are omnipotent. Nothing is beyond Your ability to work out. To overcome. So on this day, I choose to trust You when You are working in the shadows of my life. I know You have marked out a path for me. I choose to *fix my eyes on Jesus, the author and perfecter of my faith, who for the joy set before Him, endured the cross, scorning its shame, and sat down at the right hand of the throne of God.* Don't let me miss the glorious future You have for me tomorrow because today I am walking through the valley of the shadow.

For the Glory of Your Great Name . . .
Jesus. Amen.

RESPOND

Write a personal declaration from this lesson that you can carry into the coming week:

GO DEEPER

READ CHAPTER 1 FROM THE BOOK: *God Won't Leave You There: Joseph's Story.*

Turn to the next page for the Session 3 Weekly Schedule.

WEEKLY SCHEDULE

DAY 1	3-Question Study—Genesis 39:1–4
DAY 2	3-Question Study—Genesis 39:6b–8
DAY 3	3-Question Study—Genesis 39:9–12
DAY 4	3-Question Study—Genesis 39:16–20a
DAY 5	3-Question Study—Genesis 39:20b–23
DAY 6	Reflection
DAY 7	Group Discussion and Video Teaching

God Is with You . . . in Suffering and Temptation

But you, man of God, flee from all this, and pursue righteousness, godliness, faith, love, endurance and gentleness. Fight the good fight of the faith.

1 Timothy 6:11–12

PERSONAL STUDY

READ: GENESIS 39

Reading the whole chapter before studying select passages will give you helpful context and insight.

INTRODUCTION

POTIPHAR'S VISIT TO THE SLAVE MARKET was timed by God, because his eye fell on a seventeen-year old Hebrew boy. I expect many buyers were looking at Joseph[, but he was bought by Potiphar,] an important official in Pharaoh's court. [As a result Joseph entered into servitude in a house that was not frivolous, casual, sloppy or mismanaged. Instead, he was placed in Potiphar's house] which most likely meant he [not only] had decent accommodations [but also most likely learned the Egyptian language and customs. He also would have been trained as an excellent administrator while indirectly becoming familiar with Pharoh's court.]

Remember, no matter how severe your affliction is or how out of control your life seems to be or how deeply you are hurting, you are in the palm of the Lord's hand. He will guide you even if you are shackled, threatened, stuck with no possible way out, left all alone, and in pain. God has a purpose for your life, just as He had a purpose for Joseph's life.

Let's step into Joseph's story. . . .

(from *God Won't Leave You There: Joseph's Story*, pp. 26–27)

God Is with You . . . in Suffering and Temptation

STEP 1 **Read God's Word.** *(Look at the passage.)*	STEP 2 **What Does God's Word Say?** *(List the facts.)*
Genesis 39:1–4	
1 Now Joseph had been taken down to Egypt. Potiphar, an Egyptian who was one of Pharaoh's officials, the captain of the guard, bought him from the Ishmaelites who had taken him there.	
2 The LORD was with Joseph so that he prospered, and he lived in the house of his Egyptian master.	
3 When his master saw that the LORD was with him and that the LORD gave him success in everything he did,	
4 Joseph found favor in his eyes and became his attendant. Potiphar put him in charge of his household, and he entrusted to his care everything he owned.	

GOD IS WITH YOU . . . IN SUFFERING AND TEMPTATION

STEP 3

What Does God's Word Mean?

(Learn the lessons.)

STEP 4

What Does God's Word Mean in My Life?

(Listen to His voice.)

STEP 5

What Will You Do About What God Has Said?

(Live in obedient response to God's Word.)

Date: ______________________________

God Is with You . . . in Suffering and Temptation

STEP 1 **Read God's Word.** *(Look at the passage.)*	STEP 2 **What Does God's Word Say?** *(List the facts.)*
Genesis 39:6b–8	
6b Now Joseph was well-built and handsome,	
7 and after a while his master's wife took notice of Joseph and said, "Come to bed with me!"	
8 But he refused. "With me in charge," he told her, "my master does not concern himself with anything in the house; everything he owns he has entrusted to my care."	

GOD IS WITH YOU . . . IN SUFFERING AND TEMPTATION

STEP 3
What Does God's Word Mean?
(Learn the lessons.)

STEP 4
What Does God's Word Mean in My Life?
(Listen to His voice.)

STEP 5
What Will You Do About What God Has Said?
(Live in obedient response to God's Word.)

Date: ______________________________

God Is with You . . . in Suffering and Temptation

STEP 1 **Read God's Word.** *(Look at the passage.)*	STEP 2 **What Does God's Word Say?** *(List the facts.)*
Genesis 39:9–12 9 "No one is greater in this house than I am. My master has withheld nothing from me except you, because you are his wife. How then could I do such a wicked thing and sin against God?" 10 And though she spoke to Joseph day after day, he refused to go to bed with her or even be with her. 11 One day he went into the house to attend to his duties, and none of the household servants was inside. 12 She caught him by his cloak and said, "Come to bed with me!" But he left his cloak in her hand and ran out of the house.	

God Is with You . . . in Suffering and Temptation

STEP 3

What Does God's Word Mean?

(Learn the lessons.)

STEP 4

What Does God's Word Mean in My Life?

(Listen to His voice.)

STEP 5

What Will You Do About What God Has Said?

(Live in obedient response to God's Word.)

Date: ______________________________

God Is with You . . . in Suffering and Temptation

STEP 1 **Read God's Word.** *(Look at the passage.)*	STEP 2 **What Does God's Word Say?** *(List the facts.)*
Genesis 39:16–20a	
16 She kept his cloak beside her until his master came home.	
17 Then she told him this story: "That Hebrew slave you brought us came to me to make sport of me.	
18 "But as soon as I screamed for help, he left his cloak beside me and ran out of the house."	
19 When his master heard the story his wife told him, saying, "This is how your slave treated me," he burned with anger.	
20a Joseph's master took him and put him in prison, the place where the king's prisoners were confined.	

GOD IS WITH YOU . . . IN SUFFERING AND TEMPTATION

STEP 3 **What Does God's Word Mean?** *(Learn the lessons.)*	STEP 4 **What Does God's Word Mean in My Life?** *(Listen to His voice.)*

STEP 5

What Will You Do About What God Has Said?

(Live in obedient response to God's Word.)

Date: ______________________

God Is with You . . . in Suffering and Temptation

STEP 1 **Read God's Word.** *(Look at the passage.)*	STEP 2 **What Does God's Word Say?** *(List the facts.)*
Genesis 39:20b–23	
20b But while Joseph was there in the prison,	
21 the LORD was with him; he showed him kindness and granted him favor in the eyes of the prison warden.	
22 So the warden put Joseph in charge of all those held in the prison, and he was made responsible for all that was done there.	
23 The warden paid no attention to anything under Joseph's care, because the LORD was with Joseph and gave him success in whatever he did.	

GOD IS WITH YOU . . . IN SUFFERING AND TEMPTATION

STEP 3

What Does God's Word Mean?

(Learn the lessons.)

STEP 4

What Does God's Word Mean in My Life?

(Listen to His voice.)

STEP 5

What Will You Do About What God Has Said?

(Live in obedient response to God's Word.)

Date: ______________________________

GOD IS WITH YOU . . . IN SUFFERING AND TEMPTATION

PERSONAL REFLECTION

Record and journal the following from your personal study on how GOD IS WITH YOU . . . IN SUFFERING AND TEMPTATION.

The Scripture that stood out to you:

The lesson that was most meaningful to you:

The commitment you made to Live in Obedient Response to God's Word:

GOD IS WITH YOU . . . IN SUFFERING AND TEMPTATION

JESUS IN THE SHADOWS

Scan this QR code for a free bonus teaching from Anne.

Read along with Anne as you watch and listen.

John's gospel revealed that Jesus, the Creator of heaven and earth, came to His own—His "brothers"—and was rejected. (John 1:10–11) That rejection placed Him on a path of unparalleled suffering. Not even Joseph's suffering could compare.

But like Joseph, Jesus never lost His focus nor His trust in His Father. Isaiah prophetically quoted Jesus as testifying, "I have not been rebellious; I have not drawn back. I offered my back to those who beat me, my cheeks to those who pulled out my beard; I did not hide my face from mocking and spitting. Because the Sovereign LORD helps me, I will not be disgraced. Therefore have I set my face like flint, and I know I will not be put to shame." (Isaiah 50:5–7)

His path of suffering led to the cross and God's ultimate purpose for Him as the Savior of the world, the King of kings and Lord of lords. Never forget that after the cross came the crown!

Man of Sorrows, What a name!
For the Son of God who came!
Ruined sinners to reclaim.
Hallelujah! What a Savior!

(Words and music of Hymn by Philip P. Bliss, 1838–1876)

(from *God Won't Leave You There: Joseph's Story*, p. 32; Scripture is NIV 1984 with permission from Biblica)

GROUP STUDY

WELCOME TO SESSION 3 of the *God Won't Leave You There* study.

Before we watch the video lesson, let's spend some time discussing and sharing what we learned in our personal studies this past week.

Together, refer to Personal Study days 1–5 on pages 32–41.

From Step 3 (for each day)—What lesson did you learn?

From Step 4 (for each day)—What application questions did you ask yourself?

Share one "Live in Obedient Response to God's Word" you committed to this week. Refer to your Personal Reflection on page 42.

WATCH VIDEO SESSION 3— GOD IS WITH YOU . . . IN SUFFERING AND TEMPTATION

(23 MINUTES)

Use the free streaming video access code found on the inside front cover of this study guide, or play the DVD. Use this space to take notes if you like.

Anne and Rachel-Ruth share Joseph's story while spending time at the Museum of the Bible in Washington, DC.

Scripture in This Session

Genesis 39

Use this space to take notes if you like.

WRAP-UP

SHARE AS A GROUP

From the video, what was either:

a new thought ______________________________

or a challenge ______________________________

or an encouragement ______________________________

or a blessing ______________________________

CLOSING PRAYER

Beloved Savior,

Give me the strength of will to want what You want for me, more than what I want for myself. Thank You that regardless of how fierce, persistent, or attractive the temptation may be, You are with me to give me all I need to resist and run from it. Then help me to reach down deep into the suitcase of courage as I settle for nothing less than everything You want to give me.

For the glory of Your great name . . .
Jesus! Amen.

(from *God Won't Leave You There: Joseph's Story*, p. 45)

RESPOND

Write a personal declaration from this lesson that you can carry into the coming week:

GO DEEPER

READ CHAPTERS 2 AND 3 FROM THE BOOK: *God Won't Leave You There: Joseph's Story.*

Turn to the next page for the Session 4 Weekly Schedule.

WEEKLY SCHEDULE

DAY 1	3-Question Study: Genesis 40:2–5
DAY 2	3-Question Study: Genesis 40:6–8
DAY 3	3-Question Study: Genesis 40:12–14, 16a, 18–19
DAY 4	3-Question Study: Genesis 40:20–22
DAY 5	3-Question Study: Genesis 40:23
DAY 6	Reflection
DAY 7	Group Discussion and Video Teaching

God Is with You . . . In The Waiting

I remain confident of this: I will see the goodness of the LORD in the land of the living. Wait for the LORD; be strong and take heart and wait for the LORD.

Psalm 27:13–14

PERSONAL STUDY

READ: GENESIS 40

Reading the whole chapter before studying select passages will give you helpful context and insight.

INTRODUCTION

WHILE JOSEPH WAS LIVING HIS DIFFICULT LIFE in the same hopeless drudgery day after day, God was on the move! But the movement was in the shadows of his life so that he was unaware as years went by. He continued to carry out his duties in prison day after day. God had not put Joseph in prison for a few months for further refining and then released him, as if to say, "Prison time over, check. Lessons learned, check." No. Joseph was there for years with no word from the Lord, no bit of hope for freedom, no promise of a way out. He waited and waited and waited. He slept in the same dreary prison cell with the same bland food and the same prison duties that led to no advancement and no pay, all while his vibrant teens and twenties passed him by. No social gatherings or date nights. No long walks in the sunshine. No fun trips to the market. No higher education. No relaxing days at the beach. His monotonous life of gray prison walls and loneliness stretched on with little hope, if any at all. If I had been Joseph, I would have focused on my awful circumstances, curled up in a fetal position, and just given up on life. The difference is that Joseph didn't get under his circumstances. He thrived in them during what was actually a waiting period.

Let's step into Joseph's story. . . .

(from *God Won't Leave You There: Joseph's Story*, pp. 47–48)

God Is with You . . . In The Waiting

STEP 1 **Read God's Word.** *(Look at the passage.)*	STEP 2 **What Does God's Word Say?** *(List the facts.)*
Genesis 40:2–5	
2 Pharaoh was angry with his two officials, the chief cupbearer and the chief baker,	
3 and put them in custody in the house of the captain of the guard, in the same prison where Joseph was confined.	
4 The captain of the guard assigned them to Joseph, and he attended them. After they had been in custody for some time,	
5 each of the two men—the cupbearer and the baker of the king of Egypt, who were being held in prison—had a dream the same night, and each dream had a meaning of its own.	

GOD IS WITH YOU . . . IN THE WAITING

STEP 3

What Does God's Word Mean?

(Learn the lessons.)

STEP 4

What Does God's Word Mean in My Life?

(Listen to His voice.)

STEP 5

What Will You Do About What God Has Said?

(Live in obedient response to God's Word.)

Date: ______________________________

God Is with You . . . In The Waiting

STEP 1 **Read God's Word.** *(Look at the passage.)*	STEP 2 **What Does God's Word Say?** *(List the facts.)*
Genesis 40:6–8 6 When Joseph came to them the next morning, he saw that they were dejected. 7 So he asked Pharaoh's officials who were in custody with him in his master's house, "Why do you look so sad today?" 8 "We both had dreams," they answered, "but there is no one to interpret them."	

GOD IS WITH YOU . . . IN THE WAITING

STEP 3

What Does God's Word Mean?

(Learn the lessons.)

STEP 4

What Does God's Word Mean in My Life?

(Listen to His voice.)

STEP 5

What Will You Do About What God Has Said?

(Live in obedient response to God's Word.)

Date: ______________________________

God Is with You . . . In The Waiting

STEP 1 **Read God's Word.** *(Look at the passage.)*	STEP 2 **What Does God's Word Say?** *(List the facts.)*

Genesis 40:12–14, 16a, 18–19

12 "This is what it means," Joseph said to him. "The three branches are three days.

13 "Within three days Pharaoh will lift up your head and restore you to your position, and you will put Pharaoh's cup in his hand, just as you used to do when you were his cupbearer.

14 "But when all goes well with you, remember me and show me kindness; mention me to Pharaoh and get me out of this prison."

16a When the chief baker saw that Joseph had given a favorable interpretation, he said to Joseph, "I too had a dream."

18 "This is what it means," Joseph said.
"The three baskets are three days. 19
Within three days Pharaoh will lift off your head and impale your body on a pole. And the birds will eat away your flesh."

God Is with You . . . In The Waiting

STEP 3
What Does God's Word Mean?
(Learn the lessons.)

STEP 4
What Does God's Word Mean in My Life?
(Listen to His voice.)

STEP 5
What Will You Do About What God Has Said?
(Live in obedient response to God's Word.)

Date: ______________________________

God Is with You . . . In The Waiting

STEP 1 **Read God's Word.** *(Look at the passage.)*	STEP 2 **What Does God's Word Say?** *(List the facts.)*

Genesis 40:20–22

20 Now the third day was Pharaoh's
birthday, and he gave a feast for all
his officials. He lifted up the heads
of the chief cupbearer and the chief
baker in the presence of his officials:

21 He restored the chief cupbearer to
his position, so that he once again
put the cup into Pharaoh's hand—

22 but he impaled the chief baker, just
as Joseph had said to them in his
interpretation.

God Is with You . . . In The Waiting

STEP 3

What Does God's Word Mean?

(Learn the lessons.)

STEP 4

What Does God's Word Mean in My Life?

(Listen to His voice.)

STEP 5

What Will You Do About What God Has Said?

(Live in obedient response to God's Word.)

Date: ______________________________

God Is with You . . . In The Waiting

STEP 1 **Read God's Word.** *(Look at the passage.)*	STEP 2 **What Does God's Word Say?** *(List the facts.)*
Genesis 40:23 23 The chief cupbearer, however, did not remember Joseph; he forgot him.	

GOD IS WITH YOU . . . IN THE WAITING

STEP 3

What Does God's Word Mean?

(Learn the lessons.)

STEP 4

What Does God's Word Mean in My Life?

(Listen to His voice.)

STEP 5

What Will You Do About What God Has Said?

(Live in obedient response to God's Word.)

Date: ______________________________

GOD IS WITH YOU...IN THE WAITING

PERSONAL REFLECTION

Record and journal the following from your personal study on how GOD IS WITH YOU . . . IN THE WAITING.

The Scripture that stood out to you:

The lesson that was most meaningful to you:

The commitment you made to Live in Obedient Response to God's Word:

GOD IS WITH YOU . . . IN THE WAITING

JESUS IN THE SHADOWS

Scan this QR code for a free bonus teaching from Anne.

Read along with Anne as you watch and listen.

When Jesus was hanging on the cross, suffering inconceivable agony, waiting to finish His Father's work, give His life, then be raised up to glory, He thought of others. He saw His disciple John standing at the foot of the cross with His mother, Mary. He asked John to take care of her, which John did for the rest of her life. (John 19:26–27) He then turned and forgave the thief who was dying on a cross next to His own.

By His example, Jesus teaches us that one way to overcome our own suffering while waiting for deliverance is to help others in their suffering. Being considerate and kind while you seek to help someone else will get your mind off your own circumstances and will ease your own pain. As Joseph served others while waiting in prison, we see Jesus in the shadows of his life.

(from *God Won't Leave You There: Joseph's Story*, p. 57)

GROUP STUDY

WELCOME TO SESSION 4 of the *God Won't Leave You There* study.

Before we watch the video lesson, let's spend some time discussing and sharing what we learned in our personal studies this past week.

Together, refer to Personal Study days 1–5 on pages 52–61.

From Step 3 (for each day)—What lesson did you learn?

From Step 4 (for each day)—What application questions did you ask yourself?

Share one "Live in Obedient Response to God's Word" you committed to this week.
Refer to your Personal Reflection page 62.

WATCH VIDEO SESSION 4— GOD IS WITH YOU . . . IN THE WAITING

(24 MINUTES)

Use the free streaming video access code found on the inside front cover of this study guide, or play the DVD. Use this space to take notes if you like.

Anne and Rachel-Ruth share Joseph's story while spending time at the Museum of the Bible in Washington, DC.

Scripture in This Session

Genesis 40

Use this space to take notes if you like.

WRAP-UP

SHARE AS A GROUP

From the video, what was either:

a new thought ____________________

or a challenge ____________________

or an encouragement ____________________

or a blessing ____________________

CLOSING PRAYER

Lamb of God,

You waited in a woman's womb for nine months before seeing the light of day. You waited for thirty years before going public with your ministry. You waited six excruciating hours on the cross to finish the work Your Father had given You to do. You waited three days in a cold, dark tomb before rising into new life. You waited forty more days before returning to Your throne in glory. And all while waiting, You served others. You taught and healed others. You thought of others. You thought of me. Please help me to be more like You. Don't let me waste my waiting but make the most of it so that I am prepared for what comes next.

For the glory of Your great name . . .
Jesus! Amen.

(from *God Won't Leave You There: Joseph's Story*, p. 58)

RESPOND

Write a personal declaration from this lesson that you can carry into the coming week:

GO DEEPER

READ CHAPTER 4 FROM THE BOOK: *God Won't Leave You There: Joseph's Story.*

Turn to the next page for the Session 5 Weekly Schedule.

WEEKLY SCHEDULE

DAY 1	3-Question Study: Genesis 41:1, 4b, 8
DAY 2	3-Question Study: Genesis 41:9–12, 14–16
DAY 3	3-Question Study: Genesis 41:39–40
DAY 4	3-Question Study: Genesis 42:6–8
DAY 5	3-Question Study: Genesis 42:18–21
DAY 6	Reflection
DAY 7	Group Discussion and Video Teaching

God Is Guiding You . . . to Repentance and Reconciliation

"Repent then, and turn to God, so that your sins may be wiped out, that times of refreshing may come from the Lord."

Acts 3:19

PERSONAL STUDY

READ: GENESIS 41–42

Reading the chapters before studying select passages will give you helpful context and insight.

INTRODUCTION

WE KNOW WHAT . . . GUILT FEELS LIKE. It gnaws at us day and night. We can try and ignore it, blame someone else, lie about it, but the guilt just sits there like a wet blanket over our hearts, weighing us down. But guilt can be our friend. The Holy Spirit uses guilt to start us on the road to repentance, orchestrating circumstances through a sermon, a text from someone, a conversation, or something else to bring the truth to the forefront of our consciousness. When we finally bring our guilt to the Lord, . . . we may feel afraid to confess, or embarrassed [. . .] teary [. . .] ashamed, but the beauty [is] that we are coming to the Lord, not running away or trying to hide what we have done. The Lord wants us to confess exactly what it is we feel guilty about, not sugarcoat [it] or sweep [it] under the rug of rationalization or self-defense. He already knows what [it is] that has made us feel guilty. He wants to make sure we acknowledge what has produced the guilt, confess it to Him, and turn away from it. [If we do,] God is faithful to pick us up, love us, and draw us closer to Himself than ever before!

The road to repentance is not necessarily quick, proving God's amazing patience. The apostle Peter explained, "The Lord is not slow in keeping his promise, as some understand slowness. Instead he is patient with you, not wanting anyone to perish, but everyone to come to repentance." (2 Peter 3:9) The Lord wants us and even longs for us to be right with Him. [The story of] Joseph [who] worked to bring his cruel brothers to repentance dramatically illustrates that the road to repentance . . . is not [necessarily] quick or easy, but . . . it leads to great blessing, peace, and freedom. [It requires patience.]

Let's step into Joseph's story. . . .

(from *God Won't Leave You There: Joseph's Story*, pp. 83–84; Scripture is NIV 1984 with permission from Biblica)

God Is Guiding You . . . to Repentance and Reconciliation

STEP 1	STEP 2
Read God's Word. *(Look at the passage.)*	**What Does God's Word Say?** *(List the facts.)*

Genesis 41:1, 4b, 8

1 When two full years had passed,
Pharaoh had a dream: He was
standing by the Nile . . .

4b Then Pharaoh woke up.

8 In the morning his mind was
troubled, so he sent for all the
magicians and wise men of Egypt.
Pharaoh told them his dreams, but
no one could interpret them for him.

God Is Guiding You . . . to Repentance and Reconciliation

STEP 3 **What Does God's Word Mean?** *(Learn the lessons.)*	STEP 4 **What Does God's Word Mean in My Life?** *(Listen to His voice.)*

STEP 5

What Will You Do About What God Has Said?

(Live in obedient response to God's Word.)

Date: ______________________

God Is Guiding You . . . to Repentance and Reconciliation

STEP 1 **Read God's Word.** *(Look at the passage.)*	STEP 2 **What Does God's Word Say?** *(List the facts.)*

Genesis 41:9–12, 14–16

9 Then the chief cupbearer said to
Pharaoh, "Today I am reminded of
my shortcomings. 10 Pharaoh was
once angry with his servants, and he
imprisoned me and the chief baker in
the house of the captain of the guard.
11 Each of us had a dream the same
night, and each dream had a meaning
of its own. 12 Now a young Hebrew was
there with us, a servant of the captain
of the guard. We told him our dreams,
and he interpreted them for us, giving
each man the interpretation of his
dream."

14 So Pharaoh sent for Joseph, and
he was quickly brought from the
dungeon. When he had shaved and
changed his clothes, he came before
Pharaoh.

15 Pharaoh said to Joseph, "I had a
dream, and no one can interpret it. But
I have heard it said of you that when
you hear a dream you can interpret
it." 16 "I cannot do it," Joseph replied to
Pharaoh, "but God will give Pharaoh
the answer he desires."

God Is Guiding You . . . to Repentance and Reconciliation

STEP 3

What Does God's Word Mean?

(Learn the lessons.)

STEP 4

What Does God's Word Mean in My Life?

(Listen to His voice.)

STEP 5

What Will You Do About What God Has Said?

(Live in obedient response to God's Word.)

Date: ______________________

God Is Guiding You . . . to Repentance and Reconciliation

STEP 1 **Read God's Word.** *(Look at the passage.)*	STEP 2 **What Does God's Word Say?** *(List the facts.)*
Genesis 41:39–40 39 Then Pharaoh said to Joseph, "Since God has made all this known to you, there is no one so discerning and wise as you. 40 "You shall be in charge of my palace, and all my people are to submit to your orders. Only with respect to the throne will I be greater than you."	

God Is Guiding You . . . to Repentance and Reconciliation

STEP 3

What Does God's Word Mean?

(Learn the lessons.)

STEP 4

What Does God's Word Mean in My Life?

(Listen to His voice.)

STEP 5

What Will You Do About What God Has Said?

(Live in obedient response to God's Word.)

Date: ______________________

God Is Guiding You . . . to Repentance and Reconciliation

STEP 1 **Read God's Word.** *(Look at the passage.)*	STEP 2 **What Does God's Word Say?** *(List the facts.)*
Genesis 42:6–8	
6 Now Joseph was the governor of the land, the person who sold grain to all its people. So when Joseph's brothers arrived, they bowed down to him with their faces to the ground.	
7 As soon as Joseph saw his brothers, he recognized them, but he pretended to be a stranger and spoke harshly to them. "Where do you come from?" he asked. "From the land of Canaan," they replied, "to buy food."	
8 Although Joseph recognized his brothers, they did not recognize him.	

God Is Guiding You . . . to Repentance and Reconciliation

STEP 3

What Does God's Word Mean?

(Learn the lessons.)

STEP 4

What Does God's Word Mean in My Life?

(Listen to His voice.)

STEP 5

What Will You Do About What God Has Said?

(Live in obedient response to God's Word.)

Date: ______________________

God Is Guiding You . . . to Repentance and Reconciliation

STEP 1 **Read God's Word.** *(Look at the passage.)*	STEP 2 **What Does God's Word Say?** *(List the facts.)*
Genesis 42:18–21	
18 On the third day, Joseph said to them, "Do this and you will live, for I fear God:	
19 "If you are honest men, let one of your brothers stay here in prison, while the rest of you go and take grain back for your starving households.	
20 "But you must bring your youngest brother to me, so that your words may be verified and that you may not die." This they proceeded to do.	
21 They said to one another, "Surely we are being punished because of our brother. We saw how distressed he was when he pleaded with us for his life, but we would not listen; that's why this distress has come on us."	

GOD IS GUIDING YOU . . . TO REPENTANCE AND RECONCILIATION

STEP 3

What Does God's Word Mean?

(Learn the lessons.)

STEP 4

What Does God's Word Mean in My Life?

(Listen to His voice.)

STEP 5

What Will You Do About What God Has Said?

(Live in obedient response to God's Word.)

Date: ______________________________

GOD IS GUIDING YOU . . . TO REPENTANCE AND RECONCILIATION

PERSONAL REFLECTION

Record and journal the following from your personal study on how GOD IS GUIDING YOU . . . TO REPENTANCE AND RECONCILIATION.

The Scripture that stood out to you:

The lesson that was most meaningful to you:

The commitment you made to Live in Obedient Response to God's Word:

JESUS IN THE SHADOWS

Scan this QR code for a free bonus teaching from Anne.

Read along with Anne as you watch and listen.

Unlike Reuben, who was willing to give up his two sons but didn't have to, God did! He gave His one and only Son so that we might live. Like Simeon, He took our place so that we could be free. Like Joseph, He suffered, giving up heaven and fellowship with His Father to come to earth and live as a carpenter's son and be unjustly treated.

But the injustice He endured was worse than Joseph's because, in the end, the rejection He endured resulted in His gruesome death on the cross. But His story doesn't end on the cross. Jesus was raised and seated on the throne with all authority placed under His feet! He now lives to intercede for us, working in our lives as we travel the road to repentance to bring us into reconciliation with His Father. (Hebrews 7:25; Philippians 2:13)

(from *God Won't Leave You There: Joseph's Story*, p. 99)

GROUP STUDY

WELCOME TO SESSION 5 of the *God Won't Leave You There* study.

Before we watch the video lesson, let's spend some time discussing and sharing what we learned in our personal studies this past week.

Together, refer to Personal Study days 1–5 on pages 72–81.

From Step 3 (for each day)—What lesson did you learn?

From Step 4 (for each day)—What application questions did you ask yourself?

Share one "Live in Obedient Response to God's Word" you committed to this week.
Refer to your Personal Reflection on page 82.

WATCH VIDEO SESSION 5—GOD IS GUIDING YOU . . . TO REPENTANCE AND RECONCILIATION
(24 MINUTES)

Use the free streaming video access code found on the inside front cover of this study guide, or play the DVD. Use this space to take notes if you like.

Anne and Rachel-Ruth share Joseph's story while spending time at the Museum of the Bible in Washington, DC.

Scripture in This Session
Genesis 41–42

Use this space to take notes if you like.

WRAP-UP

SHARE AS A GROUP

From the video, what was either:

a new thought ______________________

or a challenge ______________________

or an encouragement ______________________

or a blessing ______________________

CLOSING PRAYER

Heavenly Dad,

This chapter has put me on the road to repentance. I'm so sorry for my sin. I confess ______________ (fill in the blank with specific sins that come to mind). I am willing to do a 180-degree turn and forsake the sin in my life. I believe Jesus died in my place on the cross. I claim His death to make atonement for my sin. Wash me clean with His blood. I believe He rose from the dead to give me eternal life, which I understand is not just a heavenly home when I die, but a personal, permanent, right relationship with You[, right now.] I receive it with thanksgiving, and I open my heart and invite Jesus to come into my life in the person of the Holy Spirit. I choose to live for Him and follow Him in obedient faith all the days of my life, right into Heaven.

For the glory of Your great name . . .
Jesus! Amen.

(from *God Won't Leave You There: Joseph's Story*, p. 100)

RESPOND

Write a personal declaration from this lesson that you can carry into the coming week:

GO DEEPER

READ CHAPTERS 5 AND 6 FROM THE BOOK: *God Won't Leave You There: Joseph's Story.*

Turn to the next page for the Session 6 Weekly Schedule.

WEEKLY SCHEDULE

DAY 1 3-Question Study: Genesis 43:24–26

DAY 2 3-Question Study: Genesis 43:32–34

DAY 3 3-Question Study: Genesis 45:1–5

DAY 4 3-Question Study: Genesis 45:15–18

DAY 5 3-Question Study: Genesis 45:25–28

DAY 6 Reflection

DAY 7 Group Discussion and Video Teaching

God Is Guiding You . . . to Forgive

For if you forgive other people when they sin against you, your heavenly Father will also forgive you.

Matthew 6:14

PERSONAL STUDY

READ: GENESIS 43–45

Reading the chapters before studying select passages will give you helpful context and insight.

INTRODUCTION

[THE TIME CAME FOR JOSEPH TO REVEAL his identity to his brothers. In that moment he had to decide if he would extend forgiveness, whether he felt like it or not. Instead of retaliating or hanging on to the temporary glory of revenge, through God's supernatural strength, Joseph chose forgiveness.]

[As he stood before them] as second-in-command of Egypt, he was able to humbly invite them, "Come close to me. . . . I am your brother Joseph, the one you sold into Egypt! And now, do not be distressed and do not be angry with yourselves for selling me here, because it was to save lives that God sent me ahead of you. . . . to preserve for you a remnant on earth and to save your lives by a great deliverance. So then, it was not you who sent me here, but God. He made me father to Pharaoh, lord of his entire household and ruler of all Egypt" (Genesis 45:4–5, 7–8).

Joseph was able to see the . . . greater purpose for which God, not the brothers, had sent him to Egypt. He reassured his brothers that the entire situation was God's plan to use him to save his family, God's chosen people, from destruction. [And it was the final step in reconciliation.]

An incredible thing happens when you and I choose to forgive: It sets us free! It also can set others free [and bring about the reconciliation we long for.]

Let's step into Joseph's story. . . .

(from *God Won't Leave You There: Joseph's Story*, pp. 156–157; Scripture is NIV 1984 with permission from Biblica)

God Is Guiding You . . . to Forgive

STEP 1 **Read God's Word.** *(Look at the passage.)*	STEP 2 **What Does God's Word Say?** *(List the facts.)*
Genesis 43:24–26	
24 The steward took the men into Joseph's house, gave them water to wash their feet and provided fodder for their donkeys.	
25 They prepared their gifts for Joseph's arrival at noon, because they had heard that they were to eat there.	
26 When Joseph came home, they presented to him the gifts they had brought into the house, and they bowed down before him to the ground.	

God Is Guiding You . . . to Forgive

STEP 3
What Does God's Word Mean?
(Learn the lessons.)

STEP 4
What Does God's Word Mean in My Life?
(Listen to His voice.)

STEP 5
What Will You Do About What God Has Said?
(Live in obedient response to God's Word.)

Date: ______________________

God Is Guiding You . . . to Forgive

STEP 1 **Read God's Word.** *(Look at the passage.)*	STEP 2 **What Does God's Word Say?** *(List the facts.)*
Genesis 43:32–34	
32 They served him by himself, the brothers by themselves, and the Egyptians who ate with him by themselves, because Egyptians could not eat with Hebrews, for that is detestable to Egyptians.	
33 The men had been seated before him in the order of their ages, from the firstborn to the youngest; and they looked at each other in astonishment.	
34 When portions were served to them from Joseph's table, Benjamin's portion was five times as much as anyone else's. So they feasted and drank freely with him.	

GOD IS GUIDING YOU . . . TO FORGIVE

STEP 3

What Does God's Word Mean?

(Learn the lessons.)

STEP 4

What Does God's Word Mean in My Life?

(Listen to His voice.)

STEP 5

What Will You Do About What God Has Said?

(Live in obedient response to God's Word.)

Date: ____________________

God Is Guiding You . . . to Forgive

STEP 1 **Read God's Word.** *(Look at the passage.)*	STEP 2 **What Does God's Word Say?** *(List the facts.)*

Genesis 45:1–5

1 Then Joseph could no longer control
himself before all his attendants, and
he cried out, "Have everyone leave
my presence!" So there was no one
with Joseph when he made himself
known to his brothers. 2 And he wept
so loudly that the Egyptians heard
him, and Pharaoh's household heard
about it.

3 Joseph said to his brothers, "I am
Joseph! Is my father still living?" But
his brothers were not able to answer
him, because they were terrified at his
presence.

4 Then Joseph said to his brothers,
"Come close to me." When they had
done so, he said, "I am your brother
Joseph, the one you sold into Egypt!

5 "And now, do not be distressed and
do not be angry with yourselves for
selling me here, because it was to save
lives that God sent me ahead of you."

God Is Guiding You . . . to Forgive

STEP 3

What Does God's Word Mean?

(Learn the lessons.)

STEP 4

What Does God's Word Mean in My Life?

(Listen to His voice.)

STEP 5

What Will You Do About What God Has Said?

(Live in obedient response to God's Word.)

Date: ______________________________

God Is Guiding You . . . to Forgive

STEP 1 **Read God's Word.** *(Look at the passage.)*	STEP 2 **What Does God's Word Say?** *(List the facts.)*
Genesis 45:15–18	
15 And he kissed all his brothers and wept over them. Afterward his brothers talked with him.	
16 When the news reached Pharaoh's palace that Joseph's brothers had come, Pharaoh and all his officials were pleased.	
17 Pharaoh said to Joseph, "Tell your brothers, 'Do this: Load your animals and return to the land of Canaan,	
18 "'and bring your father and your families back to me. I will give you the best of the land of Egypt and you can enjoy the fat of the land.'"	

GOD IS GUIDING YOU . . . TO FORGIVE

STEP 3

What Does God's Word Mean?

(Learn the lessons.)

STEP 4

What Does God's Word Mean in My Life?

(Listen to His voice.)

STEP 5

What Will You Do About What God Has Said?

(Live in obedient response to God's Word.)

Date: ______________________________

God Is Guiding You . . . to Forgive

STEP 1 **Read God's Word.** *(Look at the passage.)*	STEP 2 **What Does God's Word Say?** *(List the facts.)*
Genesis 45:25–28	
25 So they went up out of Egypt and came to their father Jacob in the land of Canaan.	
26 They told him, "Joseph is still alive! In fact, he is ruler of all Egypt." Jacob was stunned; he did not believe them.	
27 But when they told him everything Joseph had said to them, and when he saw the carts Joseph had sent to carry him back, the spirit of their father Jacob revived.	
28 And Israel said, "I'm convinced! My son Joseph is still alive. I will go and see him before I die."	

God Is Guiding You . . . to Forgive

STEP 3
What Does God's Word Mean?
(Learn the lessons.)

STEP 4
What Does God's Word Mean in My Life?
(Listen to His voice.)

STEP 5
What Will You Do About What God Has Said?
(Live in obedient response to God's Word.)

Date: ______________________________

GOD IS GUIDING YOU . . . TO FORGIVE

PERSONAL REFLECTION

Record and journal the following from your personal study on how GOD IS GUIDING YOU . . . TO FORGIVE.

The Scripture that stood out to you:

The lesson that was most meaningful to you:

The commitment you made to Live in Obedient Response to God's Word:

GOD IS GUIDING YOU . . . TO FORGIVE

JESUS IN THE SHADOWS

Scan this QR code for a free bonus teaching from Anne.

SCAN ME

Read along with Anne as you watch and listen.

What will it be like one day to stand before the Lord[, not of Egypt, but the Lord of] heaven and earth? The One under whose feet God the Father has placed all authority? With horror, dread, guilt, and shame will our eyes be riveted on His scars? Beginning at His head, will we see the wound on His brow where the crown of thorns had been embedded? As our eyes leave His brow, will they travel down to the scar on His side where the sword was thrust? And will our gaze then end at the wounds in His hands and feet where the nails had pierced Him? For the first time, we will fully comprehend the [gigantic] suffering our sin cost Him! [My sin!] His death on the cross was my fault!

Will you and I fall on our faces because our knees and legs tremble so violently [they will no longer hold us upright]? Will our voices be paralyzed into silence? We will have no excuses, defenses, rationalizations, or arguments to give. As we lie there in silence and stillness, will we feel His gentle touch on our shoulder and hear the compassion in His voice as He reassures us, *Do not be afraid. I am the First and the Last. I am the Living One; I was dead, and behold I am alive for ever and ever!* (Revelation 1:17–18)

(from *God Won't Leave You There: Joseph's Story*, p. 137; Scripture is NIV 1984 with permission from Biblica)

GROUP STUDY

WELCOME TO SESSION 6 of the *God Won't Leave You There* study.

Before we watch the video lesson, let's spend some time discussing and sharing what we learned in our personal studies this past week.

Together, refer to Personal Study days 1–5 on pages 92–101.

From Step 3 (for each day)—What lesson did you learn?

From Step 4 (for each day)—What application questions did you ask yourself?

Share one "Live in Obedient Response to God's Word" you committed to this week.
Refer to your Personal Reflection on page 102.

WATCH VIDEO SESSION 6— GOD IS GUIDING YOU . . . TO FORGIVE

(24 MINUTES)

Use the free streaming video access code found on the inside front cover of this study guide, or play the DVD. Use this space to take notes if you like.

Anne and Rachel-Ruth share Joseph's story while spending time at the Museum of the Bible in Washington, DC.

Scripture in This Session
Genesis 43–45

Use this space to take notes if you like.

WRAP-UP

SHARE AS A GROUP

From the video, what was either:

a new thought ______________________________

or a challenge ______________________________

or an encouragement ______________________________

or a blessing ______________________________

CLOSING PRAYER

Lord of lords,

Today, I bow my knee before You and confess that You are not only Lord of lords; You are my Lord. If for no other reason, I choose to forgive those who have wronged me out of my deepest gratitude for the forgiveness I have received from You. I praise You for Your great mercy, grace, and love, which I know I don't deserve. Please help me to live out my thankfulness by being a reflection of You to others. Set me free from the torturers of unforgiveness. I choose now to "just be nice."

For the glory of Your great name . . .
Jesus! Amen.

(from *God Won't Leave You There: Joseph's Story*, p. 139)

RESPOND

Write a personal declaration from this lesson that you can carry into the coming week:

GO DEEPER

READ CHAPTERS 7 AND 8 FROM THE BOOK: *God Won't Leave You There: Joseph's Story.*

Turn to the next page for the Session 7 Weekly Schedule.

WEEKLY SCHEDULE

Day 1	3-Question Study: Genesis 46:1–4
Day 2	3-Question Study: Genesis 46:28–30
Day 3	3-Question Study: Genesis 47:5–7, 11
Day 4	3-Question Study: Genesis 47:27–30
Day 5	3-Question Study: Genesis 48:15–16
Day 6	Reflection
Day 7	Group Discussion and Video Teaching

God Will Bring You Through . . . with Hope

"What no eye has
seen, what no ear
has heard, and what
no human mind has
conceived" . . . what
God has prepared for
those who love him.

1 Corinthians 2:9

PERSONAL STUDY

READ: GENESIS 46–48

Reading the chapters before studying select passages will give you helpful context and insight.

INTRODUCTION

AS YOU SEEK GOD, REMEMBER . . . Often when God wants to get a point across to us, He will speak twice. It's critical that we learn to listen to what God may be trying to tell us through repetition. When you and I are faced with a big decision . . . we need to ask God to confirm His will to us through His Word. [His confirmation brings peace and confidence so we will less likely be tempted to doubt the decision if things don't go the way we expected.] Joseph must have been filled with intense anticipation of reuniting with his family, yet he stayed focused on his responsibilities even as he waited. . . .

I wonder if his eyes kept scanning the horizon, looking for a large caravan approaching through a dusty haze. . . . When he . . . went to bed at night, did the hope of seeing his father again consume his thoughts? What would his dad look like after all these years? What would Jacob's reaction be when he saw Joseph? Would there still be a deep bond between them? Would his father be proud of the man that he had become? . . . What would it be like to have the love of a father after all these years? The long wait, the years of grief and suffering, would soon be over!

Let's step into Joseph's story. . . .

(from *God Won't Leave You There: Joseph's Story*, pp. 149–150)

GOD WILL BRING YOU THROUGH . . . WITH HOPE

STEP 1 **Read God's Word.** *(Look at the passage.)*	STEP 2 **What Does God's Word Say?** *(List the facts.)*
Genesis 46:1–4	
1 So Israel set out with all that was his, and when he reached Beersheba, he offered sacrifices to the God of his father Isaac.	
2 And God spoke to Israel in a vision at night and said, "Jacob! Jacob!" "Here I am," he replied.	
3 "I am God, the God of your father," he said. "Do not be afraid to go down to Egypt, for I will make you into a great nation there.	
4 "I will go down to Egypt with you, and I will surely bring you back again. And Joseph's own hand will close your eyes."	

God Will Bring You Through . . . with Hope

STEP 3
What Does God's Word Mean?
(Learn the lessons.)

STEP 4
What Does God's Word Mean in My Life?
(Listen to His voice.)

STEP 5
What Will You Do About What God Has Said?
(Live in obedient response to God's Word.)

Date: ______________________

God Will Bring You Through . . . with Hope

STEP 1 **Read God's Word.** *(Look at the passage.)*	STEP 2 **What Does God's Word Say?** *(List the facts.)*
Genesis 46:28–30 28 Now Jacob sent Judah ahead of him to Joseph to get directions to Goshen. When they arrived in the region of Goshen, 29 Joseph had his chariot made ready and went to Goshen to meet his father Israel. As soon as Joseph appeared before him, he threw his arms around his father and wept for a long time. 30 Israel said to Joseph, "Now I am ready to die, since I have seen for myself that you are still alive."	

GOD WILL BRING YOU THROUGH . . . WITH HOPE

STEP 3 **What Does God's Word Mean?** *(Learn the lessons.)*	STEP 4 **What Does God's Word Mean in My Life?** *(Listen to His voice.)*

STEP 5

What Will You Do About What God Has Said?

(Live in obedient response to God's Word.)

Date: ______________________

God Will Bring You Through . . . with Hope

STEP 1 **Read God's Word.** *(Look at the passage.)*	STEP 2 **What Does God's Word Say?** *(List the facts.)*
Genesis 47:5–7, 11	
5 Pharaoh said to Joseph, "Your father and your brothers have come to you,	
6 and the land of Egypt is before you; settle your father and your brothers in the best part of the land. Let them live in Goshen. And if you know of any among them with special ability, put them in charge of my own livestock."	
7 Then Joseph brought his father Jacob in and presented him before Pharaoh. After Jacob blessed Pharaoh . . .	
11 So Joseph settled his father and his brothers in Egypt and gave them property in the best part of the land, the district of Rameses, as Pharaoh directed.	

God Will Bring You Through . . . with Hope

STEP 3
What Does God's Word Mean?
(Learn the lessons.)

STEP 4
What Does God's Word Mean in My Life?
(Listen to His voice.)

STEP 5
What Will You Do About What God Has Said?
(Live in obedient response to God's Word.)

Date: ______________________________

GOD WILL BRING YOU THROUGH ... WITH HOPE

STEP 1 **Read God's Word.** *(Look at the passage.)*	STEP 2 **What Does God's Word Say?** *(List the facts.)*
Genesis 47:27–30	
27 Now the Israelites settled in Egypt in the region of Goshen. They acquired property there and were fruitful and increased greatly in number.	
28 Jacob lived in Egypt seventeen years, and the years of his life were a hundred and forty-seven.	
29 When the time drew near for Israel to die, he called for his son Joseph and said to him, "If I have found favor in your eyes, put your hand under my thigh and promise that you will show me kindness and faithfulness. Do not bury me in Egypt,	
30 "but when I rest with my fathers, carry me out of Egypt and bury me where they are buried." "I will do as you say," he said.	

GOD WILL BRING YOU THROUGH . . . WITH HOPE

STEP 3

What Does God's Word Mean?

(Learn the lessons.)

STEP 4

What Does God's Word Mean in My Life?

(Listen to His voice.)

STEP 5

What Will You Do About What God Has Said?

(Live in obedient response to God's Word.)

Date: ______________________

God Will Bring You Through . . . with Hope

STEP 1 **Read God's Word.** *(Look at the passage.)*	STEP 2 **What Does God's Word Say?** *(List the facts.)*

Genesis 48:15–16

15 Then he blessed Joseph and said,

"May the God before whom my fathers
Abraham and Isaac walked faithfully,
the God who has been my shepherd
all my life to this day,

16 "the Angel who has delivered me from all harm
—may he bless these boys.
May they be called by my name
and the names of my fathers Abraham and Isaac,
and may they increase greatly
on the earth."

GOD WILL BRING YOU THROUGH . . . WITH HOPE

STEP 3
What Does God's Word Mean?
(Learn the lessons.)

STEP 4
What Does God's Word Mean in My Life?
(Listen to His voice.)

STEP 5
What Will You Do About What God Has Said?
(Live in obedient response to God's Word.)

Date: ______________________

GOD WILL BRING YOU THROUGH . . . WITH HOPE

PERSONAL REFLECTION

Record and journal the following from your personal study on how GOD WILL BRING YOU THROUGH . . . WITH HOPE.

The Scripture that stood out to you:

The lesson that was most meaningful to you:

The commitment you made to Live in Obedient Response to God's Word:

GOD WILL BRING YOU THROUGH . . . WITH HOPE

JESUS IN THE SHADOWS

Scan this QR code for a free bonus teaching from Anne.

Read along with Anne as you watch and listen.

Jesus endured the cross, scorning its shame and humiliation, for the joy of redeeming you and me from our spiritually impoverished, sinful condition. (Hebrews 12:2) We were alienated from Him (Colossians 1:21). But through His incomprehensible suffering, brutal death, and glorious resurrection, He has reconciled us to Himself. What will it be like, at long last, after more than two thousand years, for us to see Him face-to-face? To hear His audible voice? To feel His physical touch? To be held in His strong, loving embrace?

The One who loves us and gave Himself for us has earned the right to throw open the gates to the throne room in heaven, walk right into the presence of God the Father, then present us before His glorious presence without fault and with great joy. (Jude 24) Hallelujah! He will not leave us here with less! There is much more to come!

(from *God Won't Leave You There: Joseph's Story*, p. 160)

GROUP STUDY

WELCOME TO SESSION 7 of the *God Won't Leave You There* study.

Before we watch the video lesson, let's spend some time discussing and sharing what we learned in our personal studies this past week.

Together, refer to Personal Study days 1–5 on pages 112–121.

From Step 3 (for each day)—What lesson did you learn?

From Step 4 (for each day)—What application questions did you ask yourself?

Share one "Live in Obedient Response to God's Word" you committed to this week.
Refer to your Personal Reflection on page 122.

WATCH VIDEO SESSION 7— GOD WILL BRING YOU THROUGH . . . WITH HOPE

(27 MINUTES)

Use the free streaming video access code found on the inside front cover of this study guide, or play the DVD. Use this space to take notes if you like.

Anne and Rachel-Ruth share Joseph's story while spending time at the Museum of the Bible in Washington, DC.

Scripture in This Session

Genesis 46–48

Use this space to notes if you like.

WRAP-UP

SHARE AS A GROUP

From the video, what was either:

a new thought ______________________________

or a challenge ______________________________

or an encouragement ______________________________

or a blessing ______________________________

CLOSING PRAYER

Abba Father,

You are the One from whom all blessings flow. You are the fountainhead of blessing. Please fill me until I overflow with Your blessing. I choose to live out and leave a lasting legacy, beginning right now. Today. In my own home, with my own children and grandchildren. Teach me how to speak words of blessing over them. To love them as You have loved me. I also ask You to open my eyes and heart to those in the next generation who are desperate, dry, parched for a kind word, a sweet smile, a gentle touch. Bless me to be a blessing to others.

For the glory of Your great name . . .
Jesus! Amen.

(from *God Won't Leave You There: Joseph's Story*, p. 181)

RESPOND

Write a personal declaration from this lesson that you can carry into the coming week:

GO DEEPER

READ CHAPTERS 9 AND 10 FROM THE BOOK: *God Won't Leave You There: Joseph's Story.*

Turn to the next page for the Session 8 Weekly Schedule.

WEEKLY SCHEDULE

Day 1	3-Question Study: Genesis 49:22–25
Day 2	3-Question Study: Genesis 49:29–33
Day 3	3-Question Study: Genesis 50:1–2, 4–6
Day 4	3-Question Study: Genesis 50:12–15, 19–21
Day 5	3-Question Study: Genesis 50:22, 24–26
Day 6	Reflection
Day 7	Group Discussion and Video Teaching

God Will Bring You Through . . . By His Grace

[God] has also set eternity in their heart.

Ecclesiastes 3:11 NASB

PERSONAL STUDY

READ: GENESIS 49–50

Reading the chapters before studying select passages will give you helpful context and insight.

INTRODUCTION

[JOSEPH'S] **BROTHERS NEVER FORGOT THEIR PROMISE** to take his bones back to Canaan. They must have hammered it into their descendants so they would never forget either. . . . After the death of Moses, when Joshua led the armies of Israel to defeat all of Canaan and the Israelites took possession of the land promised to Abraham, Isaac, and Jacob, finally the Bible says that "Joseph's bones, which the Israelites had brought up from Egypt, were buried at Shechem in the track of land that Jacob bought for a hundred pieces of silver from the sons of Hamor, the father of Shechem. This became the inheritance of Joseph's descendants." (Joshua 24:32) Joseph was home in Canaan at last! But, more importantly, his yearning for home one day will finally be satisfied because of his choice to place his confident hope in God. The God who had not left him in the pit, nor in Potiphar's house, nor in Pharoah's prison, nor even on the throne of Egypt. The same God who will not even leave him in a cold, dark grave in Canaan. The same God who had been with him and guided him on every step of his life's journey will bring him through to live forever in His heavenly Home.

And Joseph's God is our God. He is your God, and He will not leave us here. He will bring us through to streets of gold, gates of pearl, and a City where there will be no more death, mourning, crying, or pain, where God will wipe every tear from our eyes, where we will see our Father's face and live with Him forever! One day, He will bring us through . . . to home!

Let's step into Joseph's story. . . .

(from *God Won't Leave You There: Joseph's Story*, pp. 224–225; Scripture is NIV 1984 with permission from Biblica)

God Will Bring You Through . . . By His Grace

STEP 1 **Read God's Word.** *(Look at the passage.)*	**STEP 2** **What Does God's Word Say?** *(List the facts.)*
Genesis 49:22–25	
22 "Joseph is a fruitful vine, a fruitful vine near a spring, whose branches climb over a wall.	
23 "With bitterness archers attacked him they shot at him with hostility.	
24 "But his bow remained steady, his strong arms stayed limber because of the hand of the Mighty One of Jacob, because of the Shepherd, the Rock of Israel,	
25 "Because of your father's God, who helps you because of the Almighty, who blesses you with blessings of the skies above, blessings of the deep springs below, blessings of the breast and womb."	

God Will Bring You Through . . . By His Grace

STEP 3
What Does God's Word Mean?
(Learn the lessons.)

STEP 4
What Does God's Word Mean in My Life?
(Listen to His voice.)

STEP 5
What Will You Do About What God Has Said?
(Live in obedient response to God's Word.)

Date: ______________________________

God Will Bring You Through . . . By His Grace

STEP 1 **Read God's Word.** *(Look at the passage.)*	STEP 2 **What Does God's Word Say?** *(List the facts.)*
Genesis 49:29–33	

29 Then he gave them these
instructions: "I am about to be
gathered to my people. Bury me with
my fathers in the cave in the field of
Ephron the Hittite,

30 "the cave in the field of Machpelah,
near Mamre in Canaan, which
Abraham bought along with the field
as a burial place from Ephron the
Hittite.

31 "There Abraham and his wife Sarah
were buried, there Isaac and his wife
Rebekah were buried, and there I
buried Leah.

32 "The field and the cave in it were
bought from the Hittites."

33 When Jacob had finished giving
instructions to his sons, he drew his
feet up into the bed, breathed his last
and was gathered to his people.

God Will Bring You Through . . . By His Grace

STEP 3
What Does God's Word Mean?
(Learn the lessons.)

STEP 4
What Does God's Word Mean in My Life?
(Listen to His voice.)

STEP 5
What Will You Do About What God Has Said?
(Live in obedient response to God's Word.)

Date: ______________________________

God Will Bring You Through . . . By His Grace

STEP 1 **Read God's Word.** *(Look at the passage.)*	STEP 2 **What Does God's Word Say?** *(List the facts.)*
Genesis 50:1–2, 4–6	
1 Joseph threw himself on his father and wept over him and kissed him.	
2 Then Joseph directed the physicians in his service to embalm his father Israel. So the physicians embalmed him.	
4 When the days of mourning had passed, Joseph said to Pharaoh's court, "If I have found favor in your eyes, speak to Pharaoh for me. Tell him,	
5 "'My father made me swear an oath and said, "I am about to die; bury me in the tomb I dug for myself in the land of Canaan." Now let me go up and bury my father; then I will return."'	
6 Pharaoh said, "Go up and bury your father, as he made you swear to do."	

GOD WILL BRING YOU THROUGH . . . BY HIS GRACE

STEP 3

What Does God's Word Mean?

(Learn the lessons.)

STEP 4

What Does God's Word Mean in My Life?

(Listen to His voice.)

STEP 5

What Will You Do About What God Has Said?

(Live in obedient response to God's Word.)

Date: ______________________

God Will Bring You Through . . . By His Grace

STEP 1 **Read God's Word.** *(Look at the passage.)*	STEP 2 **What Does God's Word Say?** *(List the facts.)*

Genesis 50:12–15, 19–21

12 So Jacob's sons did as he had
commanded them: 13 They carried him
to the land of Canaan and buried him
in the cave in the field of Machpelah,
near Mamre, which Abraham had
bought along with the field as a burial
place from Ephron the Hittite.

14 After burying his father, Joseph
returned to Egypt, together with his
brothers and all the others who had
gone with him to bury his father.

15 When Joseph's brothers saw that their
father was dead, they said, "What if
Joseph holds a grudge against us and
pays us back for all the wrongs we did
to him?"

19 But Joseph said to them, "Don't be
afraid. Am I in the place of God?

20 "You intended to harm me, but God
intended it for good to accomplish what
is now being done, the saving of many
lives.

21 "So then, don't be afraid. I will provide
for you and your children." And he
reassured them and spoke kindly to
them.

God Will Bring You Through . . . By His Grace

STEP 3 **What Does God's Word Mean?** *(Learn the lessons.)*	STEP 4 **What Does God's Word Mean in My Life?** *(Listen to His voice.)*

STEP 5

What Will You Do About What God Has Said?

(Live in obedient response to God's Word.)

Date: ____________________

God Will Bring You Through . . . By His Grace

STEP 1 **Read God's Word.** *(Look at the passage.)*	STEP 2 **What Does God's Word Say?** *(List the facts.)*
Genesis 50:22, 24–26 22 Joseph stayed in Egypt, along with all his father's family. He lived a hundred and ten years. 24 Then Joseph said to his brothers, "I am about to die. But God will surely come to your aid and take you up out of this land to the land he promised on oath to Abraham, Isaac and Jacob." 25 And Joseph made the Israelites swear an oath and said, "God will surely come to your aid, and then you must carry my bones up from this place." 26 So Joseph died at the age of a hundred and ten. And after they embalmed him, he was placed in a coffin in Egypt.	

God Will Bring You Through . . . By His Grace

STEP 3
What Does God's Word Mean?
(Learn the lessons.)

STEP 4
What Does God's Word Mean in My Life?
(Listen to His voice.)

STEP 5
What Will You Do About What God Has Said?
(Live in obedient response to God's Word.)

Date: ______________________________

God Will Bring You Through . . . By His Grace

PERSONAL REFLECTION

Record and journal the following from your personal study on how GOD WILL BRING YOU THROUGH . . . BY HIS GRACE.

The Scripture that stood out to you:

The lesson that was most meaningful to you:

The commitment you made to Live in Obedient Response to God's Word:

GOD WILL BRING YOU THROUGH . . . BY HIS GRACE

JESUS IN THE SHADOWS

Scan this QR code for a free bonus teaching from Anne.

Read along with Anne as you watch and listen.

The night before His death on the cross, Jesus gathered His beloved disciples around Him in the upper room after their last supper together. He knew they were grieving at the thought of His leaving.

So one of the first things He told them was that they were not to let their hearts be troubled.

While He knew they would be plunged into the pit of extreme persecution after His departure because of their identity with Him, He instructed them to maintain their trust in Him. He told them plainly that He was going to His Father's house to prepare it for them. He was going home.

Then He gave them a promise that has lifted His followers out of the pit for the past two thousand years when He said, "I will come back and take you to be with me that you also may be where I am." (John 14:3) In essence, He was saying, "I won't leave you there!" You are going home! Jesus is coming for you! How can you know for sure? Because He said so!

(from *God Won't Leave You There: Joseph's Story*, p. 226; Scripture is NIV 1984 with permission from Biblica)

GROUP STUDY

WELCOME TO SESSION 8 of the *God Won't Leave You There* study.

Before we watch the video lesson, let's spend some time discussing and sharing what we learned in our personal studies this past week.

Together, refer to Personal Study days 1–5 on pages 132–141.

From Step 3 (for each day)—What lesson did you learn?

From Step 4 (for each day)—What application questions did you ask yourself?

Share one "Live in Obedient Response to God's Word" to which you committed to this week.

Refer to your Personal Reflection on page 142.

WATCH VIDEO SESSION 8— GOD WILL BRING YOU THROUGH . . . BY HIS GRACE

(27 MINUTES)

Use the free streaming video access code found on the inside front cover of this study guide, or play the DVD. Use this space to take notes if you like.

Anne and Rachel-Ruth share Joseph's story while spending time at the Museum of the Bible in Washington, DC.

Scripture in This Session

Genesis 49–50

Use this space to take notes if you like.

WRAP-UP

SHARE AS A GROUP

From the video, what was either:

a new thought ____________________

or a challenge ____________________

or an encouragement ____________________

or a blessing ____________________

CLOSING PRAYER

Beloved Son of the Father,

My heart aches to be with You. I yearn to go Home. The sufferings of this pit . . . make the longing so intense, I can hardly endure one more day. I need Your strength to live as Joseph lived for Your honor and glory alone. . . . I choose to die to my wants, my dreams, my goals, my aspirations, and my feelings. I lay them all down. I surrender all to Your plan and purpose for my life. In the days that are left, use me in such a way that others can see Your character reflected in me and applaud You. I choose to live with eternity in view, filled with confident hope that You won't leave me here.

For the glory of Your great name . . .
Jesus! Amen.

(from *God Won't Leave You There: Joseph's Story*, p. 227)

RESPOND

Write a personal declaration from this lesson that you can carry into the coming week:

GO DEEPER

READ CHAPTERS 11 AND 12 FROM THE BOOK: *God Won't Leave You There: Joseph's Story.*

GROUP PRAYER REQUESTS

Date: ____________________

Date: ____________________

Date: ________________

____
____
____
____
____
____
____
____

Date: ________________

____
____
____
____
____
____
____

Date: ____________________

Date: ____________________

Date: ____________________

Date: ____________________

BIBLE STUDY WORKSHOP

FOR THE BEST EXPERIENCE in facilitating this study, it's important to preview the video for session 1 and complete all the written exercises in this study guide prior to leading your group. Pray Ephesians 1:17–18 for them, that God will open their hearts to His Word, and they will get to know Him better as a result of the Spirit's revelation.

SESSION OUTLINE (90 MINUTES)

I. Introduction/Opening Prayer (5 minutes)
II. Explanation of Bible Study Sessions (5 minutes)
III. Video Teaching and Group Work (70 minutes)
  A. Opening and Teaching on Steps 1–2 (13 minutes)
  B. Group Work on Steps 1–2 (5 minutes)
  C. Review of Steps 1–2 and Teaching on Step 3 (2 minutes)
  D. Group Work on Step 3 (15 minutes)
  E. Review of Step 3 and Teaching on Step 4 (13 minutes)
  F. Group Work on Step 4 (5 minutes)
IV. Wrapping Up and Next Steps (10 minutes)

INTRODUCTION/OPENING PRAYER
(5 MINUTES)

Take a few moments as this opening session begins to introduce yourself to anyone in the group you do not know and give your contact information. If it can be done quickly, ask the participants to introduce themselves. It may be helpful in a larger group to provide nametags. To save time, you can have the nametags pre-printed with their names on one side, and your name and contact information on the other side. Ensure the participants have a copy of the study guide. Pray that God would use the coming hour to help everyone present to become more effective students and doers of His Word.

EXPLANATION OF BIBLE STUDY SESSIONS
(5 MINUTES)

Explain that this first session in *God Won't Leave You There* is unique, as Anne and Rachel-Ruth will describe a method for studying the Bible that they will use during their personal quiet time throughout the study. During this opening session, which will be approximately 90 minutes in length, the group members will watch the video and complete the work found on pages 1–7.

VIDEO TEACHING AND GROUP WORK
(70 MINUTES)

Show the video, following the instructions given during the session. Note that you will be stopping the video periodically for the participants to complete each of the steps.

WRAPPING UP AND NEXT STEPS
(10 MINUTES)

Tell the group members that they will begin to explore how God is always with you in sessions 2–8. Refer group members to the Personal Bible Study found on pages 6–7 and ask them to complete the studies before the next session. Close your time in prayer.

GOD IS WITH YOU . . . FROM THE BEGINNING

PREVIEW THE VIDEO BEFORE YOUR MEETING and complete all the written exercises in this guide. Familiarize yourself with the session outline and gather the necessary materials. Remember also to pray for the participants who will be attending.

SESSION OUTLINE
(60 MINUTES)

REVIEW OF PERSONAL STUDY (20 MINUTES)

Welcome any new participants, and then refer the group to their notes on pages 12–23. Begin by having several different members share the following:

- The lessons they learned from each verse (Step 3)
- The most meaningful question they wrote out in response to Step 4, citing the verse on which the question was based
- Their outstanding takeaway in Step 5

VIDEO TEACHING (25 MINUTES)

Watch the teaching video for Session 2. Refer the group members to page 25 and remind them there is space to take notes.

WRAP-UP, PRAYER, RESPOND, AND GO DEEPER (15 MINUTES)

Share as a group reflections on the topics presented during the video teaching, any personal encouragement, challenge, or inspiration they received as they watched.

Respond with a personal declaration.

Conclude by praying over your group. Review the next week's schedule on page 28. Remind them to complete the personal studies before the next session.

God Is with You . . . in Suffering and Temptation

Preview the video before your meeting and complete all the written exercises in this guide. Familiarize yourself with the session outline and gather the necessary materials. Remember also to pray for the participants who will be attending.

SESSION OUTLINE
(60 MINUTES)

REVIEW OF PERSONAL STUDY (20 MINUTES)

Welcome any new participants, and then refer the group to their notes on pages 32–43. Begin by having several different members share the following:

- The lessons they learned from each verse (Step 3)
- The most meaningful question they wrote out in response to Step 4, citing the verse on which the question was based
- Their outstanding takeaway in Step 5

VIDEO TEACHING (25 MINUTES)

Watch the teaching video for Session 3. Refer the group members to page 45 and remind them there is space to take notes.

WRAP-UP, PRAYER, RESPOND, AND GO DEEPER (15 MINUTES)

Share as a group reflections on the topics presented during the video teaching, any personal encouragement, challenge, or inspiration they received as they watched.

Respond with a personal declaration.

Conclude by praying over your group. Review the next week's schedule on page 48. Remind them to complete the personal studies before the next session.

God Is with You . . . In The Waiting

Preview the video before your meeting and complete all the written exercises in this guide. Familiarize yourself with the session outline and gather the necessary materials. Remember also to pray for the participants who will be attending.

SESSION OUTLINE
(60 MINUTES)

REVIEW OF PERSONAL STUDY (20 MINUTES)

Welcome any new participants, and then refer the group to their notes on pages 52–63. Begin by having several different members share the following:

- The lessons they learned from each verse (Step 3)
- The most meaningful question they wrote out in response to Step 4, citing the verse on which the question was based
- Their outstanding takeaway in Step 5

VIDEO TEACHING (25 MINUTES)

Watch the teaching video for Session 4. Refer the group members to page 65 and remind them there is space to take notes.

WRAP-UP, PRAYER, RESPOND, AND GO DEEPER (15 MINUTES)

Share as a group reflections on the topics presented during the video teaching, any personal encouragement, challenge, or inspiration they received as they watched.

Respond with a personal declaration.

Conclude by praying over your group. Review the next week's schedule on page 68. Remind them to complete the personal studies before the next session.

God Is Guiding You . . . to Repentance and Reconciliation

Preview the video before your meeting and complete all the written exercises in this guide. Familiarize yourself with the session outline and gather the necessary materials. Remember also to pray for the participants who will be attending.

SESSION OUTLINE
(60 MINUTES)

REVIEW OF PERSONAL STUDY (20 MINUTES)

Welcome any new participants, and then refer the group to their notes on pages 72–83. Begin by having several different members share the following:

- The lessons they learned from each verse (Step 3)
- The most meaningful question they wrote out in response to Step 4, citing the verse on which the question was based
- Their outstanding takeaway in Step 5

VIDEO TEACHING (25 MINUTES)

Watch the teaching video for Session 5. Refer the group members to page 85 and remind them there is space to take notes.

WRAP-UP, PRAYER, RESPOND, AND GO DEEPER (15 MINUTES)

Share as a group reflections on the topics presented during the video teaching, any personal encouragement, challenge, or inspiration they received as they watched.

Respond with a personal declaration.

Conclude by praying over your group. Review the next week's schedule on page 88. Remind them to complete the personal studies before the next session.

God Is Guiding You . . . to Forgive

Preview the video before your meeting and complete all the written exercises in this guide. Familiarize yourself with the session outline and gather the necessary materials. Remember also to pray for the participants who will be attending.

Session Outline (60 Minutes)

Review of Personal Study (20 minutes)

Welcome any new participants, and then refer the group to their notes on pages 92–103. Begin by having several different members share the following:

- The lessons they learned from each verse (Step 3)
- The most meaningful question they wrote out in response to Step 4, citing the verse on which the question was based
- Their outstanding takeaway in Step 5

VIDEO TEACHING (25 MINUTES)

Watch the teaching video for Session 6. Refer the group members to page 105 and remind them there is space to take notes.

WRAP-UP, PRAYER, RESPOND, AND GO DEEPER (15 MINUTES)

Share as a group reflections on the topics presented during the video teaching, any personal encouragement, challenge, or inspiration they received as they watched.

Respond with a personal declaration.

Conclude by praying over your group. Review the next week's schedule on page 108. Remind them to complete the personal studies before the next session.

GOD WILL BRING YOU THROUGH . . . WITH HOPE

PREVIEW THE VIDEO BEFORE YOUR MEETING and complete all the written exercises in this guide. Familiarize yourself with the session outline and gather the necessary materials. Remember also to pray for the participants who will be attending.

SESSION OUTLINE
(60 MINUTES)

REVIEW OF PERSONAL STUDY (20 MINUTES)

Welcome any new participants, and then refer the group to their notes on pages 112–123. Begin by having several different members share the following:

- The lessons they learned from each verse (Step 3)
- The most meaningful question they wrote out in response to Step 4, citing the verse on which the question was based
- Their outstanding takeaway in Step 5

VIDEO TEACHING (25 MINUTES)

Watch the teaching video for Session 7. Refer the group members to page 125 and remind them there is space to take notes.

WRAP-UP, PRAYER, RESPOND, AND GO DEEPER (15 MINUTES)

Share as a group reflections on the topics presented during the video teaching, any personal encouragement, challenge, or inspiration they received as they watched.

Respond with a personal declaration.

Conclude by praying over your group. Review the next week's schedule on page 128. Remind them to complete the personal studies before the next session.

God Will Bring You Through . . . By His Grace

Preview the video before your meeting and complete all the written exercises in this guide. Familiarize yourself with the session outline and gather the necessary materials. Remember also to pray for the participants who will be attending.

SESSION OUTLINE
(60 MINUTES)

REVIEW OF PERSONAL STUDY (20 MINUTES)

Welcome any new participants, and then refer the group to their notes on pages 132–143. Begin by having several different members share the following:

- The lessons they learned from each verse (Step 3)
- The most meaningful question they wrote out in response to Step 4, citing the verse on which the question was based
- Their outstanding takeaway in Step 5

VIDEO TEACHING (25 MINUTES)

Watch the teaching video for Session 8. Refer the group members to page 145 and remind them there is space to take notes.

WRAP-UP, PRAYER, RESPOND, AND GO DEEPER (15 MINUTES)

Share as a group reflections on the topics presented during the video teaching, any personal encouragement, challenge, or inspiration they received as they watched.

Respond with personal declaration.

Conclude by praying over your group.

Also By Anne and Rachel-Ruth

JESUS FOLLOWERS VIDEO BIBLE STUDY

Join Anne Graham Lotz and Rachel-Ruth Lotz Wright for this five-session study as they demonstrate a family Bible study discussion, plus four ways to ignite faith in the next generation, centered around your Witness, Worship, Walk, and Work. Intentionally following Jesus in these aspects of your daily life will make you more effective as you seek to ignite faith in the next generation.

JESUS FOLLOWERS BOOK

Drawing on the fascinating genealogy of Genesis 5, Anne explores the unique impact of our witness worship, work, and walk. Rachel-Ruth illustrates these elements with stories from the Graham and Lotz families of how God's truth was passed on by word and example.

VIDEO BIBLE STUDIES Also By
Anne Graham Lotz

EXPECTING TO SEE JESUS

In this nine-session small group Bible study, Anne Graham Lotz delivers a new message from the Mount of Olives in Israel and issues a wake-up call using the signs of Jesus' return.

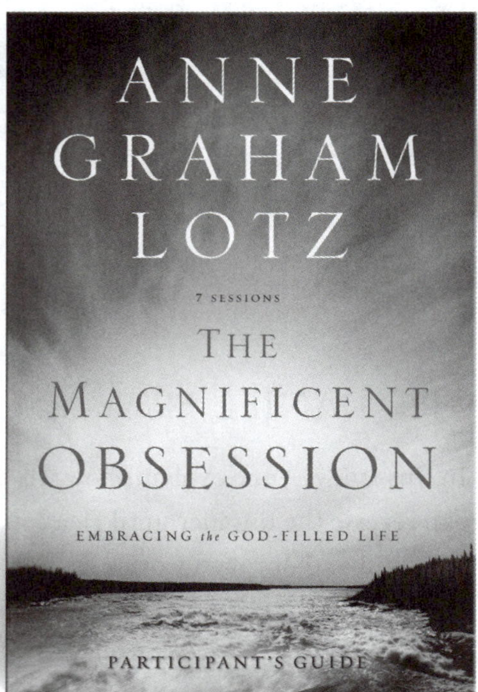

MAGNIFICENT OBSESSION

Follow author Anne Graham Lotz in this seven-session small group video Bible study, on a journey through Abraham's life, and learn—as he did—how to live a life of joy and purpose in the midst of struggle and doubt.